DIGITAL GOVERNMENT:

BUILDING A 21ST CENTURY PLATFORM TO BETTER SERVE THE AMERICAN PEOPLE

MAY 23, 2012

Table of Contents

Introduction

"I want us to ask ourselves every day, how are we using technology to make a real difference in people's lives." —President Barack Obama

Mission drives agencies, and the need to deliver better services to customers at a lower cost—whether an agency is supporting the warfighter overseas, a teacher seeking classroom resources or a family figuring out how to pay for college—is pushing every level of government to look for new solutions.

Today's amazing mix of cloud computing, ever-smarter mobile devices, and collaboration tools is changing the consumer landscape[1] and bleeding into government as both an opportunity and a challenge. New expectations require the Federal Government to be ready to deliver and receive digital information[2] and services[3] anytime, anywhere and on any device. It must do so safely, securely, and with fewer resources. To build for the future, the Federal Government needs a Digital Strategy that embraces the opportunity to innovate more with less, and enables entrepreneurs to better leverage government data to improve the quality of services to the American people.

Early mobile adopters in government—like the early web adopters—are beginning to experiment in pursuit of innovation. Some have created products that leverage the unique capabilities of mobile devices. Others have launched programs and strategies and brought personal devices into the workplace. Absent coordination, however, the work is being done in isolated, programmatic silos within agencies.

Building for the future requires us to think beyond programmatic lines. To keep up with the pace of change in technology, we need to securely architect our systems for interoperability and openness from conception. We need to have common standards and more rapidly share the lessons learned by early adopters. We need to produce better content and data, and present it through multiple channels in a program and device-agnostic[4] way. We need to adopt a coordinated approach to ensure privacy and security in a digital age.

---

1. Source for "The Speed of Digital Information": http://mashable.com/2011/08/23/virginia-earthquake/. Sources for "The Rapidly Changing Mobile Landscape": http://hugin.info/1061/R/1561267/483187.pdf, http://www.idc.com/getdoc.jsp?containerId=prUS23028711, http://pewinternet.org/Reports/2012/Smartphone-Update-2012/Findings.aspx, http://tech.fortune.cnn.com/2011/02/07/idc-smartphone-shipment-numbers-passed-pc-in-q4-2010/.
2. Digital information is information that the government provides digitally. Information, as defined in OMB Circular A-130, is any communication or representation of knowledge such as facts, data, or opinions in any medium or form, including textual, numerical, graphic, cartographic, narrative, or audiovisual forms. See http://www.whitehouse.gov/omb/circulars_a130_a130trans4 for more information.
3. Digital services include the delivery of digital information (i.e. data or content) and transactional services (e.g. online forms, benefits applications) across a variety of platforms, devices and delivery mechanisms (e.g. websites, mobile applications, and social media).
4. Device-agnostic means a service is developed to work regardless of the user's device, e.g. a website that works whether viewed on a desktop computer, laptop, smartphone, media tablet or e-reader.

These imperatives are not new, but many of the solutions are. We can use modern tools and technologies to seize the digital opportunity and fundamentally change how the Federal Government serves both its internal and external customers—building a 21st century platform to better serve the American People.

> **The Rapidly Changing Mobile Landscape**
>
> - Mobile broadband subscriptions are expected to grow from nearly 1 billion in 2011 to over 5 billion globally in 2016.
>
> - By 2015, more Americans will access the Internet via mobile devices than desktop PCs.
>
> - As of March 2012, 46% of American adults were smartphone owners – up from 35% in May 2011.
>
> - In 2011, global smartphone shipments exceeded personal computer shipments for the first time in history.

Strategy Objectives

The Digital Government Strategy sets out to accomplish three things:

- **Enable the American people and an increasingly mobile workforce to access high-quality digital government information and services anywhere, anytime, on any device.**

  Operationalizing an information-centric model, we can architect our systems for interoperability and openness, modernize our content publication model, and deliver better, device-agnostic digital services at a lower cost.

- **Ensure that as the government adjusts to this new digital world, we seize the opportunity to procure and manage devices, applications, and data in smart, secure and affordable ways.**

  Learning from the previous transition of moving information and services online, we now have an opportunity to break free from the inefficient, costly, and fragmented practices of the past, build a sound governance structure for digital services, and do mobile "right" from the beginning.

- **Unlock the power of government data to spur innovation across our Nation and improve the quality of services for the American people.**

  We must enable the public, entrepreneurs, and our own government programs to better leverage the rich wealth of federal data to pour into applications and services by ensuring that data is open and machine-readable by default.

About this Document

The Digital Government Strategy complements several initiatives aimed at building a 21st century government that works better for the American people. These include Executive Order 13571 (Streamlining Service Delivery and Improving Customer Service),[5] Executive Order 13576 (Delivering an Efficient, Effective, and Accountable Government),[6] the President's Memorandum on Transparency and Open Government,[7] OMB Memorandum M-10-06 (Open Government Directive),[8] the National Strategy for Trusted Identities in Cyberspace (NSTIC),[9] and the 25-Point Implementation Plan to Reform Federal Information Technology Management (IT Reform).[10]

Through IT Reform, the Federal Government has made progress in foundational execution areas such as adopting "light technologies" (e.g. cloud computing), shared services (e.g. commodity IT), modular approaches for IT development and acquisition, and improved IT program management. The strategy leverages this progress while focusing on the next key priority area that requires government-wide action: *innovating with less to deliver better digital services*. It specifically draws upon the overall approach to increase return on IT investments, reduce waste and duplication, and improve the effectiveness of IT solutions defined in the Federal Shared Services Strategy.[11]

The Digital Government Strategy incorporates a broad range of input from government practitioners, the public, and private-sector experts. Two cross-governmental working groups—the Mobility Strategy and Web Reform Task Forces—provided guidance and recommendations for building a digital government. These groups worked with the Office of Management and Budget (OMB) and General Services Administration (GSA) to conduct current state research (e.g. the December 2011 State of the Federal Web Report[12]) and explore solutions for the future of government digital services. Feedback was also incorporated from citizens and federal workers across the nation using online public dialogues, including the September 2011 *National Dialogue on Improving Federal Websites* and the January 2012 *National Dialogue on the Federal Mobility Strategy* which produced a combined total of 570 ideas and nearly 2,000 comments.[13]

---

5. http://www.whitehouse.gov/the-press-office/2011/04/27/executive-order-streamlining-service-delivery-and-improving-customer-ser
6. http://www.whitehouse.gov/the-press-office/2011/06/13/executive-order-13576-delivering-efficient-effective-and-accountable-gov
7. http://www.whitehouse.gov/sites/default/files/omb/assets/memoranda_2010/m10-06.pdf
8. http://www.whitehouse.gov/the_press_office/Transparency_and_Open_Government
9. http://www.whitehouse.gov/sites/default/files/rss_viewer/NSTICstrategy_041511.pdf
10. http://www.cio.gov/documents/25-Point-Implementation-Plan-to-Reform-Federal%20IT.pdf
11. http://www.cio.gov/documents/Shared_Services_Strategy.pdf
12. The State of the Federal Web Report, released in December 2011, was created based on agency-provided information and can be found at http://www.usa.gov/webreform/state-of-the-web.pdf.
13. The National Dialogues are archived at http://web-reform-dialogue.ideascale.com/ (Improving Federal Websites) and http://mobility-strategy.ideascale.com/ (Federal Mobility Strategy).

Conceptual Model

Before discussing *how* we will build a 21st century digital government, we must first establish a conceptual model that acknowledges the three "layers" of digital services (see Figure 1).

The ***information layer*** contains digital information. It includes structured information (e.g., the most common concept of "data") such as census and employment data, plus unstructured information (e.g., content), such as fact sheets, press releases, and compliance guidance.[14]

The ***platform layer*** includes all the systems and processes used to manage this information. Examples include systems for content management, processes such as web API (Application Programming Interface)[15] and application development, services that support mission critical IT functions such as human resources or financial management, as well as the hardware used to access information (e.g., mobile devices).

The ***presentation layer*** defines the manner in which information is organized and provided to customers. It represents the way the government and private sector deliver government information (e.g., data or content) digitally, whether through websites,[16] mobile applications, or other modes of delivery.

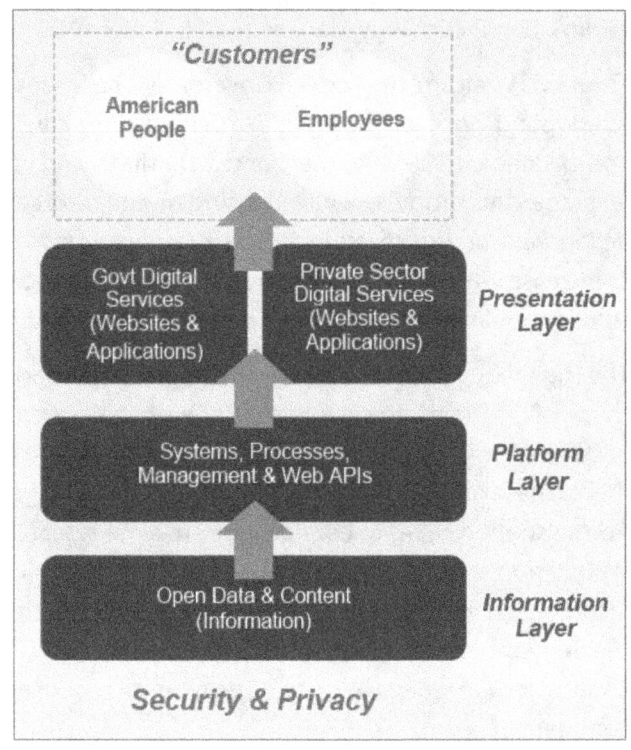

Figure 1: The Layers of Digital Services

These three layers separate information *creation* from information *presentation*—allowing us to create content and data once, and then use it in different ways. In effect, this model represents a fundamental shift from the way our government provides digital services today.

---

14. For the purposes of this document, the term "content" will refer to all unstructured information, while the term "data" will refer to all structured information unless otherwise noted.

15. Web APIs are a system of machine-to-machine interaction over a network. Web APIs involve the transfer of data, but not a user interface.

16. A website is the hosted content on a domain, which has a unique homepage and global navigation, e.g., NASA.gov is a domain, but www.nasa.gov and jpl.nasa.gov are both websites on that domain.

Strategy Principles

To drive this transformation, the strategy is built upon four overarching principles:

- An *"**Information-Centric**"* approach—Moves us from managing "documents" to managing discrete pieces of open data and content[17] which can be tagged, shared, secured, mashed up and presented in the way that is most useful for the consumer of that information.

- A *"**Shared Platform**"* approach—Helps us work together, both within and across agencies, to reduce costs, streamline development, apply consistent standards, and ensure consistency in how we create and deliver information.

- A *"**Customer-Centric**"* approach—Influences how we create, manage, and present data through websites, mobile applications, raw data sets, and other modes of delivery, and allows customers to shape, share and consume information, whenever and however they want it.

- A platform of *"**Security and Privacy**"*—Ensures this innovation happens in a way that ensures the safe and secure delivery and use of digital services to protect information and privacy.

Information-Centric

The Federal Government must fundamentally shift how it thinks about digital information. Rather than thinking primarily about the final presentation—publishing web pages, mobile applications or brochures—an information-centric approach focuses on ensuring our data and content are accurate, available, and secure. We need to treat all content as data[18]—turning any unstructured content into structured data—then ensure all structured data are associated with valid metadata.[19] Providing this information through web APIs helps us architect for interoperability and openness, and makes data assets freely available for use within agencies, between agencies, in the private sector, or by citizens. This approach also supports device-agnostic security and privacy controls, as attributes can be applied directly to the data and monitored through metadata, enabling agencies to focus on securing the data and not the device.

---

17. Open data and content for the purposes of this document refers to digital information that is structured and exposed in a way that makes it accessible for meaningful use beyond its system of origin, be that internal to the government or external to the public. This builds upon the definition of "openness" in OMB Memorandum M-10-06 (Open Government Directive), which specifically addresses the release of information to the public: "Agencies shall respect the presumption of openness by publishing information online…To the extent practicable and subject to valid restrictions, agencies should publish information online in an open format that can be retrieved, downloaded, indexed, and searched by commonly used web search applications. An open format is one that is platform independent, machine readable, and made available to the public without restrictions that would impede the re-use of that information." See http://www.whitehouse.gov/open/documents/open-government-directive for more information.
18. To treat content as data and turn unstructured content into structured data, web-based documents must be created as pieces of structured information. For example, a fact sheet may be broken into the following component data pieces: the title, body text, images, and related links.
19. Metadata are information used to describe certain attributes of a piece of digital information, such as page title, author, date updated, and other classifications. Consistent quality metadata tagging can improve search results and also be used to structure content so that it can be more widely disseminated.

In production, the information-centric approach ensures all agencies follow the same "rules of the road" by using open standards. It also guides how we present information, from mobile applications to websites, and allows for increased automation at the presentation layer. If done right, the information-centric approach will add reach and value to government services by helping to surface the best information and making it widely available through a variety of useful formats.

Shared Platform

To make the most use of our resources and *"innovate with less"*, we need to share more effectively, both within the government and with the public. We also need to share capacities to build the systems and processes that support our efforts, and be smart about creating new tools, applications, systems, websites and domains. Ultimately, a shared platform approach to developing and delivering digital services and managing data not only helps accelerate the adoption of new technologies, but also lowers costs and reduces duplication. To do so, we need to rapidly disseminate lessons learned from early adopters, leverage existing services and contracts, build for multiple use cases at once, use common standards and architectures, participate in open source communities, leverage public crowdsourcing, and launch shared government-wide solutions and contract vehicles.[20]

Customer-Centric

From how we create information, to the systems we use to manage it, to how we organize and present it, we must focus on our customers' needs. Putting the customer first means quality information is accessible, current and accurate at any time whether the customer is in the battle field, the lab, or the classroom. It means coordinating across agencies to ensure when citizens and employees interact with government information and services, they can find what they need and complete transactions with a level of efficiency that rivals their experiences when engaging with the private-sector.

The customer-centric principle charges us to do several things: conduct research to understand the customer's business, needs and desires; make content more broadly available and accessible and present it through multiple channels in a program- and device-agnostic way; make content more accurate and understandable by maintaining plain language and content freshness standards; and offer easy paths for feedback to ensure we continually improve service delivery. The customer-centric principle holds true whether our customers are internal (e.g. the civilian and military federal workforce in both classified and unclassified environments) or external (e.g. individual citizens, businesses, research organizations, and state, local, and tribal governments).

Security and Privacy

As the Federal Government builds for the future, it must do so in a safe and secure, yet transparent and accountable manner. Architecting for openness and adopting new technologies have the potential to make devices and data vulnerable to malicious or accidental breaches of security and privacy. They also

---

20. A shared solution is a service such as web hosting, application support, or a content management system, provided by a single agency or organization, but used by many. For example, a central hosting platform that allows multiple agencies to host their web content rather than procuring separate infrastructure for each new project.

create challenges in providing adequate notice of a user's rights and options when providing personally identifiable information (PII).

Moving forward, we must strike a balance between the very real need to protect sensitive government and citizen assets given the realities of a rapidly changing technology landscape. To support information sharing and collaboration, we must build in security, privacy, and data protection throughout the entire technology life cycle. To promote a common approach to security and privacy, we must streamline assessment and authorization processes, and support the principle of "do once, use many times". We must also adopt new solutions in areas such as continuous monitoring, identity, authentication, and credential management, and cryptography that support the shift from securing devices to securing the data itself and ensure that data is only shared with authorized users. When appropriate, requirements and solutions should be collaboratively developed with industry to match Federal Government needs, using the power of innovation and economies of scale to deliver better-value security and privacy products.

Part A. Information-Centric

The rich wealth of information maintained by the Federal Government is a national asset with tremendous potential value to the public, entrepreneurs, and to our own government programs. This information takes many forms. It can be unstructured content (e.g. press releases, help documents, or how-to guides) or more structured data (e.g. product safety databases, census results, or airline on-time records). Regardless of form, to harness its value to the fullest extent possible, we must adopt an information-centric approach to digital services by securely architecting for interoperability and openness from the start.

Traditionally, the government has architected systems (e.g. databases or applications) for specific uses at specific points in time. The tight coupling of presentation and information has made it difficult to extract the underlying information and adapt to changing internal and external needs. This has necessarily resulted in a duplication of efforts and the building of multiple systems to serve different audiences where a single would suffice. For example, most websites are typically built with webpages sized specifically for computer screens. To serve mobile audiences, many agencies build an entirely new mobile site to present the same content to federal employees and the public.

An information-centric approach decouples information from its presentation. It means beginning with the data or content,[21] describing that information clearly, and then exposing it to other computers in a machine-readable format—commonly known as providing web APIs. In describing the information, we need to ensure it has sound taxonomy (making it searchable) and adequate metadata (making it authoritative). Once the structure

> **Decoupling Data and Presentation**
>
> The Centers for Disease Control and Prevention (CDC) is liberating web content by decoupling data and presentation. Using a "create once, publish everywhere mindset" and an API-driven syndication service, CDC's content flows easily into multiple channels and is available for public and private reuse. Within its own channels, content is updated once, and then easily displayed on the main CDC.gov web site, the mobile site at m.cdc.gov, and in the various modules of the CDC mobile app.
>
> In 2011, CDC's liberated content was syndicated to 700 registered partners in all 50 US states, the District of Columbia and 15 countries and accounted for an additional 1.2 million page views.

of the information is sound, various mechanisms can be built to present it to customers (e.g. websites, mobile applications, and internal tools) or raw data can be released directly to developers and entrepreneurs outside the organization. This approach to opening data and content means organizations can consume the same web APIs to conduct their day-to-day business and operations as they do to provide services to their customers.

In addition, by embedding security and privacy controls into structured data and metadata, data owners can focus more effort on ensuring the safe and secure delivery of data to the end customer and fewer resources on securing the device that will receive the data. For example, security of an endpoint device

---

21. Unstructured content like web-based fact sheets must be broken into their component data pieces (e.g. the title, body text, images, and related links) and treated as structured data.

becomes less of a risk management factor if data is protected and authorized users must authenticate their identities to gain access to it.

The private sector has proven an information-centric model for delivering digital services securely and efficiently. The time has come for the Federal Government to embrace this approach in stride. Recognizing that simply publishing snapshots of government information is not enough to make it open, we need to improve the quality, accessibility, timeliness, and usability of our data and content through well-defined standards that include the use of machine-readable formats such as web APIs and common metadata tagging schemas.

1. Make Open Data, Content, and Web APIs the New Default

To lay the foundation for opening data and content efficiently, effectively and accessibly, OMB will work with representatives from across government to develop and publish an open data, content, and web API policy for the Federal Government. This policy will leverage central coordination and leadership to develop guidelines, standards, and best practices for improved interoperability. To establish a "new default," the policy will require that newly developed IT systems are architected for openness and expose high-value[22] data and content as web APIs at a discrete and digestible level of granularity with metadata tags[23]. Under a presumption of openness, agencies must evaluate the information contained within these systems for release to other agencies and the public, publish it in a timely manner, make it easily accessible for external use as applicable, and post it at agency.gov/developer in a machine-readable format.

> **Fueling the App Economy**
>
> The City of San Francisco releases its raw public transportation data on train routes, schedules, and to-the-minute location updates directly to the public through web services. This has enabled citizen developers to write over 10 different mobile applications to help the public navigate San Francisco's public transit systems—more services than the city could provide if it focused on presentation development rather than opening the data publicly through web services.

#	Owner(s)	Milestone Actions	Timeframe (months)			
			1	3	6	12
1.1	OMB	Issue government-wide open data, content, and web API policy and identify standards and best practices for improved interoperability.			•	
1.2	Agencies	Ensure all new IT systems follow the open data, content, and web API policy and operationalize agency.gov/developer pages. *[Within 6 months of release of open data policy— see milestone 1.1]*				•

---

22. High-value information is information that can be used to increase agency accountability and responsiveness; improve public knowledge of the agency and its operations; further the core mission of the agency; create economic opportunity; or respond to need and demand as identified through public consultation.
23. Industry-standard markup language (e.g. XBRL, XML) will be used to the extent practicable.

2. Make Existing High-Value Data and Content Available through Web APIs

Recognizing that change will not happen overnight, we need to adopt an efficient and cost effective implementation strategy that will not place an undue burden on agencies to transition all existing systems and information upfront. While the open data and web API policy will apply to all new systems and underlying data and content developed going forward, OMB will ask agencies to bring existing high-value systems and information into compliance over a period of time—a *"look forward, look back"* approach. To jump-start the transition, agencies will be required to:

- Identify at least two major customer-facing systems that contain high-value data and content;
- Expose this information through web APIs to the appropriate audiences;
- Apply metadata tags in compliance with the new federal guidelines; and
- Publish a plan to transition additional systems as practical.

Given the scope, scale, and complexity of some of these systems, agencies will be asked to prioritize release of data and content so the most valuable information is made available first. In cases where the system supports a website, content must also be structured, published through web APIs and tagged appropriately. Agencies will be required to engage with their customers[24] within three months to identify the highest priority systems to transition, and work internally across communications, content, and infrastructure teams (e.g. program leads, digital strategists, web managers, Chief Information Officers (CIOs), Chief Financial Officers (CFOs), Chief Technology Officers (CTOs), Chief Acquisition Officers (CAOs), Chief Public Affairs Officers, Geographic Information Officers (GIOs), and data managers to select the final candidates. GSA will help agencies develop web APIs through the Digital Services Innovation Center (see section 3). Additionally, Data.gov will be expanded to include a web API catalog to serve as an interactive directory of information made available to the public by agencies via web services so that customers may more readily utilize that information in their own applications. Web APIs posted on agencies'/developer pages will be automatically aggregated in this catalog.

#	Owner(s)	Milestone Actions	Timeframe (months)			
			1	3	6	12
2.1	Agencies	Engage with customers to identify at least two existing major customer-facing services that contain high-value data or content as first-move candidates to make compliant with new open data, content, and web API policy.		•		
2.2	Agencies	Make high-value data and content in at least two existing major customer-facing systems available through web APIs, apply metadata tagging and publish a plan to transition additional high-value systems. *[Within 6 months of release of open data policy—see milestone 1.1]*				•
2.3	GSA	Expand Data.gov to include a web API catalog that centrally aggregates web APIs posted on agencies'/developer pages.				•

---

24. Customers may be internal (e.g. the civilian and military federal workforce in both classified and unclassified environments) or external (e.g. individual citizens, businesses, research organizations, and state, local, and tribal governments.) Agencies with external customers should engage the public.

Part B. Shared Platform

Government agencies are missing out on opportunities to share ideas and resources within the digital services space.[25] Inefficiencies such as fragmented procurement and development practices waste taxpayer dollars and stymie the consistent adoption of new technologies and approaches. The shift to a shared platform culture will require strong leadership at the government-wide and agency levels. Agencies must begin to look first to shared solutions and existing infrastructure when developing new projects, rather than procuring new infrastructure and systems for each new project. They must also share ownership of common service areas, both within and across agencies, instead of creating multiple websites on the same topic. To alleviate the burden on individual agencies, prevent duplication, and spur innovation, we must provide central support for the adoption of new technologies, development of better digital services, and strengthening of governance.

> **Opportunities to Share**
>
> In the State of the Federal Web Report, agencies reported 150 separate implementations of 42 different systems used to create and publish content and 250 web hosting providers.

3. Establish a Digital Services Innovation Center and Advisory Group

There are common challenges that all agencies face in trying to deliver better digital services at a lower cost to the American people and employees. Approaching these challenges as one government will enable agencies to focus their time and money on developing innovative, mission-facing solutions rather than re-inventing the wheel.

Identifying opportunities for sharing existing solutions at agencies and building new solutions for government-wide use requires strong leadership, coordination, and support. To operationalize the principle of *"build once, use many times"*, GSA will expand its current efforts and establish a Digital Services Innovation Center. The Center will work with agencies to establish shared solutions and training to support infrastructure and content needs across the Federal Government (e.g. source code sharing tools, video captioning, language translation, usability and accessibility testing, web hosting, and security architectures). The Innovation Center will support agencies lacking these capabilities, not supersede agencies' existing capabilities, and function as a cooperative enterprise that draws on resources from across government and leverages the expertise of forward-leaning agencies.

At the outset, to support strategy implementation, the Center will focus on three initial actions:

- **Identify shared and open content management system (CMS) solutions** and support implementation through training and best practices. This will offer agencies an alternative to building their own platforms in isolation and enable code sharing and modular development.

- **Help agencies develop web APIs** and unlock valuable data by providing expert resources and other support to enable developers, entrepreneurs, and other end users take advantage of government data and content.

---

25. The State of the Federal Web Report provides several examples. See http://www.usa.gov/webreform/state-of-the-web.pdf for more information.

- **Launch a shared mobile application development program,** in conjunction with the Federal CIO Council, that will help agencies develop secure, device-agnostic mobile applications, provide a development test environment to streamline app delivery, foster code-sharing, and validate official government applications.

To augment the natural cross-agency collaboration that has developed through initiatives such as the Web Reform and Mobility Strategy Task Forces, OMB will formalize and sustain such coordination into the future by convening a Digital Services Advisory Group that draws membership from the Federal CIO Council, Federal Web Managers Council, and other agency leaders. Through its leadership, the Advisory Group will promote cross-agency sharing and accelerated adoption of mobile workforce solutions and best practices in the development and delivery of digital services that build in security and privacy and keep the federal workforce abreast of emerging technologies. Overall, in addition to advising the Federal CIO on implementation of the strategy, the Advisory Group will have three main focus areas:

- **Help prioritize shared services needs for the Digital Services Innovation Center.** The Advisory Group will identify areas that need government-wide leadership and work with the Innovation Center to determine the best shared solutions that leverage existing agency work and commercial options to the extent practical.

- **Foster the sharing of existing policies and best practices** using online platforms and communities of practice to provide more structure to existing ad-hoc collaboration efforts. For instance, many front-running agencies have already launched bring-your-own-device (BYOD) pilots that test new devices and solutions. The Advisory Group will work with the Federal CIO Council to develop government-

---

The Need for Open Content Management Solutions

According to the State of the Federal Web Report, over 43% of federal agencies currently do not use CMS solutions for publishing content online. In many cases, the lack of CMS means maintaining and updating websites is an inefficient, manual process.

A prominent theme from the National Dialogue on Improving Federal Websites was the need to phase out the use of custom-built technology. Participants in the dialogue recommended that the Federal Government use open source technology to enable more sharing of data and make content more accessible. *"Encourage use of popular Open Source platforms"* was one of the many ideas submitted in this vein and generated robust discussion.

Creating an Environment for Mobility

A popular idea submitted during the National Dialogue on the Federal Mobility Strategy got straight to the point: *"Apps are easy… enterprise strategy, not so much."* As one commenter put it, we need to look at *"how mobility (not just mobile technology) fits into an organization, regardless of the device, platform, application, etc."*

"Mobility" is not just about embracing the newest technology, but rather reflects a fundamental change in how, when, and where our citizens and employees work and interact. Mobile technology—the devices, infrastructure, and applications required to support a mobile citizenry and workforce—is a critical enabler of mobility, but is only part of the profound environmental shift that mobility represents.

wide BYOD guidance leveraging their findings. The Advisory Group will also work with the Federal Web Managers Council to develop guidelines for improving digital services and creating better digital content (see section 6) and setting up intra-agency governance models for delivering better digital services (see section 4).

- **Identify and recommend changes to help close gaps in policy and standards.** For instance, as new technologies are introduced into the federal environment, policies governing identity and credential management may need to be revised to allow the introduction of new solutions that work better in a mobile world. Equally, as new technologies emerge, telework rules may need to be revisited to allow employees to work from any location, as long as the device and connectivity are appropriately secure.

#	Owner(s)	Milestone Actions	Timeframe (months)			
			1	3	6	12
3.1	GSA	Establish a Digital Services Innovation Center to improve the government's delivery of digital services.	•			
3.2	OMB	Convene a Digital Services Advisory Group to provide input on priorities for the Innovation Center activities and recommend government-wide best practices, guidance, and standards.	•			
3.3	Advisory Group/Federal CIO Council	Release government-wide bring-your-own-device (BYOD) guidance based on lessons learned from successful pilots at federal agencies.		•		
3.4	Innovation Center	Identify shared and open content management system solutions.			•	
3.5	Innovation Center	Provide support to help agencies develop web APIs.			•	
3.6	Innovation Center/ Federal CIO Council	Launch a shared mobile app development program.				•

4. Establish Intra-Agency Governance to Improve Delivery of Digital Services

At the agency-level, Agency CIOs are responsible[26] for commodity IT services and information security. However, the lines of responsibility for developing and delivering content and data are not as clear and distinct. Agencies must decide how they will staff and manage the delivery of digital services across the enterprise. An uncoordinated approach at some agencies has resulted in the development and maintenance of dozens—in some cases hundreds—of separate websites and supporting infrastructure, and

---

26. To clarify the role of Chief Information Officers (CIO), the Director of the OMB issued OMB Memorandum M-11-29 (Chief Information Officer Authorities) to the heads of Executive Departments and Agencies. In addition to their statutory responsibilities through the Clinger-Cohen Act and related laws, Agency CIOs have a lead role in four main areas: IT Governance, Commodity IT, Program Management, and Information Security. OMB continues to work with Congress to consolidate Commodity IT spending under the Agency CIO.

application of varying degrees of quality and fiscal control to these resources. In many cases, agencies lack consistent processes to measure performance and ensure content quality.

Agencies must drive better decision-making across the organization about how best to spend resources on digital services and manage their data. The Digital Services Advisory Group (see section 3) will recommend guidelines to help agencies set up an effective governance structure where it does not yet exist. The guidance will suggest a range of approaches, but not prescribe specific structures, and set expectations for activities and outcomes. For example, as agencies establish new governance structures or strengthen existing ones, they will be required to establish specific, measurable goals for delivering better services at a lower cost (e.g. through domain consolidation) and set agency-wide standards for content lifecycle management, adoption of third-party online tools, mobile application delivery, and sharing (e.g. infrastructure and digital information).

#	Owner(s)	Description and Milestone Actions	Timeframe (months)			
			1	3	6	12
4.1	Advisory Group	Recommend guidelines on agency-wide governance structure for developing and delivering digital services and managing data.		•		
4.2	Agencies	Establish an agency-wide governance structure for developing and delivering digital services. *[Within 3 months of release of governance guidance—see milestone 4.1]*			•	

5. Shift to an Enterprise-Wide Asset Management and Procurement Model

Traditionally, agencies have purchased technology products and services in a fragmented manner at the bureau, regional, team, and even individual levels.[27] This approach has prevented the Federal Government from effectively leveraging its buying power with vendors and service providers. In the mobile space alone, the opportunity to increase efficiencies and cut costs is too great to overlook. The Federal Government currently spends approximately $1.2 billion annually for mobile and wireless services and devices with an inventory of approximately 1.5 million active accounts.[28] These figures will only increase as agencies accelerate their adoption of new mobile technologies.

By moving to an enterprise-wide model, we can leverage economies of scale and streamline purchasing,

Fragmented...

Three separate federal agencies located in Atlanta pay three different monthly service plan rates for unlimited data on the same type of device—$39, $94, and $120—a significant price variance of $81.

...and Centralized

In 2011, the United States Department of Agriculture (USDA) centralized its wireless procurement by collapsing over 700 separate contracts into three blanket purchase agreements (BPA), resulting in acquisition cost savings of 18%.

invoicing, and asset management processes. We can also explore different pricing models, such as usage-based pricing (e.g. metered), first at the agency-wide level and eventually at the government-wide level.

---

27. For a broader treatment of this issue, refer to the Federal Shared Services Strategy.

28. Figures on mobile spending, including call-out box, drawn from research of the Federal Strategic Sourcing Initiative. See http://www.gsa.gov/portal/content/105156 for more information.

Adopting a shared services approach and consolidating mobile device and wireless service contracts will not only reduce costs but also improve our ability to track usage, analyze pricing, secure devices, and deliver mobile applications. This is in line with the Administration's overall effort to consolidate the acquisition and management of commodity IT services[29] through mechanisms such as the Federal Strategic Sourcing Initiative, the PortfolioStat process[30], and the Administrative Efficiency Initiative.[31]

To jumpstart this shift, GSA will establish a government-wide contract vehicle for mobile devices and wireless service and offer agencies the option of accessing central portal services for placing orders, reporting inventory, and managing expenses to optimize their mobile usage. GSA will also set up a government-wide mobile device management platform to support enhanced monitoring, management, security, and device synchronization. The Federal CIO Council will work with the Digital Services Advisory Group (see Section 3) to develop models for the secure, yet rapid, delivery of commercial mobile applications into the federal environment to support the consistent application of security and interoperability requirements. For example, an enterprise mobile application environment could provide central hosting, distribution, certification, and management services for mobile applications.

For their part, agencies will be required to develop and maintain an enterprise-wide inventory of their mobile devices and wireless service contracts, and include an evaluation of government-wide contract vehicles in their alternatives analysis for all new mobile-related procurements.

#	Owner(s)	Milestone Actions	Timeframe (months)			
			1	3	6	12
5.1	GSA	Establish government-wide contract vehicle for mobile devices and wireless service.			•	
5.2	Agencies	Develop an enterprise-wide inventory of mobile devices and wireless service contracts.			•	
5.3	Agencies	Evaluate the government-wide contract vehicles in the alternatives analysis for all new mobile-related procurements.				•
5.4	Advisory Group/ Federal CIO Council	Develop models for the delivery of commercial mobile applications into the federal environment.				•
5.5	GSA	Set up a government-wide mobile device management platform.				•

29. Examples of commodity IT services identified in OMB Memorandum M-11-29 include IT Infrastructure (e.g. Data Centers, Networks, Desktop Computers, Mobile Devices), Enterprise IT Systems (e.g. E-mail, Collaboration Tools, Identity and Access Management, Security, Web Infrastructure), Business Systems (e.g. Finance, Human Resources, Other Administrative Functions).

30. Under OMB Memorandum M-12-10 (Implementing PortfolioStat), agency Chief Operating Officers (COO) are required to lead an annual agency-wide IT portfolio review (PortfolioStat) to reduce duplication within commodity IT by shifting to intra- and inter-agency shared services. This includes acquisitions for acquiring mobile devices, applications, and wireless telecommunications services. See http://www.whitehouse.gov/sites/default/files/omb/memoranda/2012/m-12-10.pdf for more information.

31. In support of the Administrative Efficiency Initiative, Executive Order 13589 (Promoting Efficient Spending) asks agencies to assess current employee device inventories and usage and establish controls to ensure that they are not paying for unused or underutilized IT equipment, installed software, or services. This includes limiting the number of devices (e.g., mobile phones, tablets) issued to employees. See http://www.whitehouse.gov/the-press-office/2011/11/09/executive-order-promoting-efficient-spending for more information.

Part C. Customer-Centric

The quality of digital services that we provide determines our reputation and trust as an institution. It profoundly affects the customer experience that our employees and citizens have in working for, and engaging with, the Federal Government. Digital services include the delivery of digital information and transactional services (e.g. online forms, benefits applications, timecard submissions) across a variety of platforms, devices and delivery mechanisms (e.g. websites, mobile applications, and social media). Regardless of the form they take, these digital services must be designed and delivered with customer service first in mind and reflect the technologies used by today's customers.

Customer-centric government means that agencies respond to customers' needs and make it easy to find and share information and accomplish important tasks.

> **Absorbing the Complexity of the Government**
>
> A common theme from the National Dialogue for Improving Federal Websites was that the Federal Government needs to change to a culture of customer service. A key part of that shift is the need to start absorbing the complexity of the Government on behalf of the citizen. As one participant wrote, *"Customers don't know—and don't care to know—how government is organized. So why make them go from agency [website] to agency [website] to get the full picture of what gov't has to offer on any subject?"*

It requires holding ourselves to a high-standard of timely data, informative content, simple transactions, and seamless interactions that are easily accessible. The mantra of *"anytime, anywhere, any device,"* is increasingly setting the standard for how information and services are both delivered and received in a two-way exchange of information and ideas. We must embrace the ability of new technologies to drive participation in the digital public square. To develop innovative, transparent, customer-facing products and services efficiently and effectively, the Federal Government must also focus on the fundamentals of customer-centric design: measure how well we are providing meaningful services; focus our efforts on those interactions that have the most use and value; institutionalize performance measurement; and continuously improve services in response to those measurements.

6. Deliver Better Digital Services Using Modern Tools and Technologies

Using modern tools and technologies such as responsive web design[32] and search engine optimization[33] is critical if the government is to adapt to an ever-changing digital landscape and deliver services to any device, anytime, anywhere. Similarly, optimizing content for modern platforms, rather than just translating content from paper-based documents to the Web, will help ensure the American people and employees can access content regardless of platform. Agencies will need to keep current with the latest design concepts and refresh content delivery mechanisms to ensure the highest performance. To help achieve these objectives, the Digital Services Advisory Group (see section 3) will work with

---

32. Responsive web design is a method of designing content so that it can be re-sized to fit on various screen sizes (e.g. designing a service to work well on both a laptop screen and a smartphone, without the need to design and maintain separate "standard" and "mobile" sites).

33. Search engine optimization involves understanding how search engines work and designing content around those standards to boost content's ranking in search results.

the Federal Web Managers Council to recommend guidelines for improving digital services and the customer experience that will set a new default for how digital services are developed and delivered. These guidelines will include:

- Approaches for consolidating duplicative websites and coordinating information delivery across agencies;

- Best practices for identifying and optimizing top tasks[34], content, and transactions, including use of plain language; optimizing for usability, search, and accessibility[35]; and implementing content lifecycle management;

- Best practices for standards-compliant, next-generation web development, including use of content delivery networks; content management systems; common code libraries, frameworks, and tools; and responsive web design (e.g. using HTML5[36] and CSS3[37] to provide a mobile-tailored experience);

- Standards for structuring and tagging content and data to be machine-readable;

- Approaches for using customer feedback to make improvements; and

- Considerations to support the adoption of an information-centric security model.

The dot gov domain guidance and procedures will be updated to help ensure all new digital services meet these improvement guidelines. Under the principle of "no new domains", criteria for approving new second-level domains will be strengthened and new domains will only be granted on an exception basis. For example, an agency may be granted a new single domain to host consolidated content previously spread across multiple domains, thus streamlining the customer experience and reducing redundant infrastructure. Domains will be approved or renewed only if they to comply with web-related federal standards, guidance, and regulations (e.g. adoption of the aforementioned guidelines, IPv6[38], DNSSEC, continuous monitoring, and externally-issued credentials[39]). In addition, the dot gov domain

---

34. Top tasks are the things customers most often try to accomplish when accessing an organization's services, whether finding specific information or completing some transaction (e.g. filing taxes).

35. Section 508 of the Rehabilitation Act of 1973 requires that federal employees and members of the public with disabilities have access to the government's digital information and services comparable to individuals without disabilities, unless an undue burden would be imposed on the agency. See http://www.access-board.gov/508.htm for more information.

36. HTML5 is the fifth revision of the Hypertext Markup Language standard used to code content for the Web. HTML5 makes it possible to embed video, audio, animations and other features without the use of third-party plugins and can be used to build cross-platform mobile applications.

37. CSS3 is the current standard for Cascading Style Sheets, a language used to specify look and feel of digital content, and used separately from the markup language (e.g., HTML) so as to separate content from presentation.

38. The Federal Acquisition Regulation (FAR) requires all new information technology acquisitions using Internet Protocol (IP) to include IPv6 requirements expressed using the USGv6 Profile and to require vendors to document their compliance with those requirements through the USGv6 Testing Program. Agencies shall institute processes to include language in solicitations and contracts, where applicable. For additional information, a copy of the September 2010 memorandum and IPv6 Frequently Asked Questions can be found at www.cio.gov.

39. The list of externally-issued credential providers that have been certified as being in accordance with government-wide requirements is at http://www.idmanagement.gov/pages.cfm/page/ICAM-TrustFramework-IDP (for non-PKI solutions) and at http://www.idmanagement.gov/pages.cfm/page/Federal-PKI-Management-Authority-entities-crosscertified-with-the-FBCA (for PKI solutions). These are the only externally-issued credentials which may be accepted. See Federal CIO Memorandum on Requirements for Accepting Externally-Issued Identity Credentials http://www.cio.gov/documents/OMBReqforAcceptingExternally_IssuedIdCred10-6-2011.pdf for more information.

registration process will reinforce existing policies prohibiting the use of non-.gov (e.g. .org, .com) top-level domains.[40] Through the Digital Services Innovation Center (see section 3), GSA will provide tools, guidelines, and training to help agencies comply with these new policies and continue efforts to consolidate websites along topical lines.

#	Owner(s)	Milestone Actions	Timeframe (months)			
			1	3	6	12
6.1	Advisory Group/ Federal Web Managers Council	Recommend guidelines for improving digital services and customer experience.			•	
6.2	GSA	Update the dot gov domain guidance and procedures to help ensure all new digital services meet improvement guidelines and provide support to agencies.			•	
6.3	Agencies	Ensure all new digital services follow digital services and customer experience improvement guidelines. *[Within 6 months of release of improvement guidance—see milestone 6.2]*				•

7. Improve Priority Customer-Facing Services for Mobile Use

The general public and our government workforce should be able to access government information and services on demand and on any device. To jump-start the transition to mobile platforms, agencies will be required to mobile-enable at least two priority customer-facing services within the next 12 months. This includes services currently provided offline or optimizing those currently delivered online for mobile platforms. Agencies will also be required to deliver information in new ways that fully harness the power and potential of mobile and web-based technologies and ensure that all domains (e.g. www. agency.gov) can be easily accessed and used on mobile devices. GSA will help coordinate these efforts to prevent the development of duplicative services and support the use of shared solutions to provide the best quality mobile services at the lowest costs (see section 3).

Agencies will be required to engage their customers within three months to identify the highest priority services to optimize for mobile use, and work internally across communications, content, and infrastructure teams to select their final candidates. They will also be required to publish a plan for improving additional existing services as practical.

#	Owner(s)	Milestone Actions	Timeframe (months)			
			1	3	6	12
7.1	Agencies	Engage with customers to identify at least two existing priority customer-facing services to optimize for mobile use.		•		
7.2	Agencies	Optimize at least two existing priority customer-facing services for mobile use and publish a plan for improving additional existing services. *[Within 6 months of release of digital services improvement guidance—see milestone 6.2]*				•

---

40. See OMB Memorandum M-05-04 (Policies for Federal Agency Public Websites) http://www.whitehouse.gov/sites/default/files/omb/memoranda/fy2005/m05-04.pdf for more information.

8. Measure Performance and Customer Satisfaction to Improve Service Delivery

Objective performance measures should drive the development and delivery of effective digital government services. Today most agencies lack enterprise-wide performance measures to consistently evaluate the success and usability of their websites. This limits their ability to allocate resources effectively to invest in critical-needs areas. Similarly, the lack of a government-wide view of performance for digital service delivery makes it difficult to properly address gaps or duplications in services.

To enable data-driven decisions on service performance, agencies will be required to use analytics and customer satisfaction measurement tools on all .gov websites within 6 months. To help these efforts, the Digital Services Innovation Center (see Section 3) will identify common tools for agencies to use that will enable aggregation of this data at the federal level. Common tools will give us the ability—for the first time—to take a government-wide view of how well we serve our customers and opens up new possibilities for consolidating and improving the federal web space and the growing number of mobile services.

Measuring Performance

According to the State of the Federal Web Report, only 10% of the 24 major federal agencies use the same performance metrics to consistently evaluate websites agency-wide. But there's a solution for that: *"Open web analytics for all .gov websites"*, a popular idea submitted during the National Dialogue on Improving Federal Websites.

#	Owner(s)	Milestone Actions	Timeframe (months)			
			1	3	6	12
8.1	Innovation Center	Identify tools and guidance for measuring performance and customer satisfaction on digital services.		•		
8.2	Agencies	Implement performance and customer satisfaction measuring tools on all .gov websites. *[Within 3 months of release of tools and guidance—see milestone 8.1]*			•	

Part D. Security and Privacy

The information maintained by the Federal Government needs to be secured regardless of how data is stored, processed, or transmitted. As information and devices become increasingly mobile, we must ensure confidentiality, integrity, and availability by building security into digital government services. As the government moves to an information-centric and mobility-enabled digital environment, existing security, privacy, and data protections[41] and cyber security priorities[42]—including Trusted Internet Connection (TICs), continuous monitoring, and strong authentication consistent with NSTIC and Federal Identity Credential and Access Management (ICAM) requirements—must be considered throughout the entire life cycle of existing and emerging technologies as part of agencies' overall organizational risk management.[43] They must also be updated to reflect the realities of a rapidly changing technology landscape.

Mobile devices have unique security challenges. Due to their portability, they are easy to misplace, potentially compromising any unencrypted sensitive data or applications stored locally. Wireless connectivity allows users to bypass an agency's secure TIC and connect directly to the Internet and other untrusted resources. These problems are not new, as the introduction of laptops into the workforce led to security and data breaches as employees took their electronic devices mobile. However, the new class of smaller, lighter smartphones and media tablets has elevated exposure to this risk. The rate of change of mobile operating systems, new update and notification capabilities from external hardware and software vendors, diversity of the devices themselves, and introduction of employee-owned devices (BYOD) also make security in the mobile space more challenging than in a traditional desktop environment and require new approaches to continuously monitor and manage devices and secure the data itself.

The challenge extends beyond the workforce and into the delivery of services to external customers. When deploying applications and other mobile technologies to interact with citizens and businesses, the Federal Government will need to foster trust, accountability, and transparency about how user information is collected, used, shared, and secured, without unduly burdening the robust development of such technologies or the user experience.

---

41. All existing federal requirements for data protection and remote access are applicable to mobile devices. For example, the security requirements in the Federal Information Security Management Act of 2002 (FISMA), OMB Circular A-130, NIST FIPS 140-2, NIST FIPS 199, and NIST FIPS 200, apply (including appropriate security and privacy controls specified in NIST Special Publication 800-53). Agencies should specify security requirements during the acquisition process and ensure that procurements capture the requirements of the Federal Acquisition Regulation (e.g. 52.225-5, Trade Agreements), OMB policy (e.g. OMB Memorandum M-06-16 and OMB Memorandum M-07-16), and NIST standards and guidelines.
42. See http://goals.performance.gov/goals_2013 for more information on the Cross-Agency Priority Goal for Cybersecurity.
43. Organizational Risk Management is a key element in an organization's information security program. A risk-based approach to securing information technology involves categorizing an information system and the information in that system based on an impact analysis, then selecting and implementing appropriate security controls. See http://csrc.nist.gov/groups/SMA/fisma/framework.html for more information.

9. Promote the Safe and Secure Adoption of New Technologies

Agencies need to continue to integrate effective security and privacy measures into the design and adoption of all new technologies introduced to the federal environment, including mobile devices, applications, and wireless networks, consistent with existing policies, and incorporate commercial security and privacy capabilities by default, augmenting controls and policies as required. To enable agencies to share security testing information and prevent unnecessary duplication, the Department of Homeland Security (DHS) and the Department of Defense (DOD) will work with the National Institute of Standards and Technology (NIST) to develop a security baseline within 12 months that provides standardized security requirements for mobile and wireless adoption in the Federal Government. This will include the development of mobile and wireless security reference architectures that incorporate security and privacy by design while accounting for different agencies' mission needs. For example, the Federal Government's evolving enterprise wireless networks may have varying needs to support unclassified and classified high-bandwidth traffic, mission critical wireless coverage to in-building and terrestrial environments, and data offloading. A government-wide mobile and wireless security baseline will enable adoption of the "do once, use many times" approach to mobile and wireless security assessment, authorization, and continuous monitoring.

Going forward, we must pilot, document, and rapidly scale new approaches to secure data and mobile technologies and address privacy concerns (see section 3 for role of the Digital Services Advisory Group in facilitating this process). Such pilots and documentation will help advance our security posture and communicate the Federal Government's expectations on product capabilities to the private sector. Shifting to the cloud is one area of opportunity. For example, if applications, operating systems, and data reside in an appropriately secured[44] cloud environment rather than on a device, this will limit the potential impact to an agency in the event a device is lost, stolen, or compromised. Other opportunity areas include adopting advanced mobile device management solutions to support continuous monitoring, strengthening identity and access management, and accepting externally-issued credentials on public-facing websites.

#	Owner(s)	Milestone Actions	Timeframe (months)			
			1	3	6	12
9.1	DHS/DOD/NIST	Develop government-wide mobile and wireless security baseline (includes security reference architectures.)				•

10. Evaluate and Streamline Security and Privacy Processes

Given the realities of a rapidly changing technology landscape, we must continually evaluate current processes for adopting new technologies and ensuring they provide security and privacy protections. As part of its ongoing work on securing mobile devices, applications, and platforms to support wider mobile adoption across the Federal Government, NIST will review existing standards and guidelines to ensure they are sufficiently flexible to accommodate mobile technology. The Federal CIO Council's

---

44. Cloud services authorized through the Federal Risk and Authorization Management Program (FedRAMP) will meet standardized security requirements and address cybersecurity priorities such as continuous monitoring and TIC. See www.FedRAMP.gov for more information.

Information Security and Identity Management Committee will also evaluate opportunities to accelerate the secure adoption mobile technologies into the federal environment at reduced costs.

As good stewards of data security and privacy, the Federal Government must ensure that there are safeguards to prevent the improper collection, retention, use or disclosure of sensitive data such as personally identifiable information (PII).[45] These safeguards should be regularly reviewed and updated as technology use, capability, and architectures advance so they do not unnecessarily stifle the government's ability to architect for openness and engage with the public. The Federal CIO Council's Privacy Committee will work with NIST and the National Archives and Records Administration (NARA) to develop guidelines for standardized implementation of privacy controls in a digital environment and educate key agency privacy and legal officials on the latest technology advances and options for addressing digital privacy (e.g. data collection and individual notice) as well as records retention and security issues.

#	Owner(s)	Milestone Actions	Timeframe (months)			
			1	3	6	12
10.1	NIST	Report on NIST's ongoing work in mobile technology, including the applicability of NIST's standards and guidelines to mobile devices and platforms.		●		
10.2	Advisory Group/ Federal CIO Council	Evaluate opportunities to accelerate the secure adoption of mobile technologies into the federal environment at reduced cost.			●	
10.3	Federal CIO Council/NIST/ NARA	Develop guidelines for standardized implementation of digital privacy controls and educate agency privacy and legal officials on options for addressing digital privacy, records retention, and security issues.			●	

---

45. For example, commercial Identity Providers approved for use under the Federal ICAM initiative have gone through a certification process to ensure that their solutions support federal privacy and security rules. See http://www. idmanagement.gov/pages.cfm/page/ICAM for more information.

Conclusion

Technology is fundamentally transforming how we conduct our business and live our daily lives. Exponential advances in computing power, the rise of high-speed networks, and the growing mobile revolution, which puts the entire Internet at our fingertips, have unleashed new innovations, spawned new industries and reshaped existing ones. The President has charged us with harnessing the power of technology to help create a 21st century digital government—one that is efficient, effective and focused on improving the delivery of services to the American people.

The roadmap actions outlined within this Digital Government Strategy form a series of critical next steps to help build a 21st century government that innovates with less. To put us on a path to unlock the potential of a digital government, the strategy emphasizes several key objectives.

First, we must enable citizens and an increasingly mobile federal workforce to securely access high-quality digital government information, data and services—*"anywhere, anytime, on any device."* By operationalizing an information-centric model, we can help agencies securely architect systems for interoperability and openness. Doing so will allow agencies to modernize their content publication model and deliver better, device-agnostic digital services at a lower cost. In addition, by providing machine-readable connections to government data and services, government agencies, businesses, and independent innovators can directly access the building blocks of government—recombining them to create new services or connecting them with existing services to streamline operations.

Secondly, we must ensure that as the government adjusts to this new digital world, we build the modern infrastructure needed to support digital government efforts and leverage the Federal Government's buying power to reduce costs. Taking what we have learned from the previous transition in moving government information and services online, we now have a chance to do mobile *"right"* from the beginning by procuring and managing devices, applications, and data in a smart, secure, and affordable manner. Establishing a Digital Services Innovation Center and Advisory Group will help lay the foundation for a well-coordinated approach toward these objectives.

Ultimately, this strategy aims to be disruptive. It provides a platform to fundamentally shift how government connects with, and provides services to, the American people. It gives the federal workforce the tools needed to carry out their mission of delivering services to all citizens—whether to a warfighter in the field retrieving geospatial imagery information; a medical researcher sharing the latest bio specimen data sets for a rare form of cancer; or a rural farmer accessing a real-time forecast of seasonal precipitation. It creates a space for citizens to become partners in building a better government, where *"every man,"* as Thomas Jefferson once wrote, *"feels that he is a participator in the government of affairs."*

Appendix: Roadmap Milestones

The following table captures all milestones in the Digital Government Strategy.

#	Owner(s)	Milestone Actions	Timeframe (months)			
			1	3	6	12
Part A: Information-Centric						
1. Make Open Data, Content, and Web APIs the New Default						
1.1	OMB	Issue government-wide open data, content, and web API policy and identify standards and best practices for improved interoperability.			•	
1.2	Agencies	Ensure all new IT systems follow the open data, content, and web API policy and operationalize agency.gov/developer pages. *[Within 6 months of release of open data policy—see milestone 1.1]*				•
2. Make Existing High-Value Data and Content Available through Web APIs						
2.1	Agencies	Engage with customers to identify at least two existing major customer-facing services that contain high-value data or content as first-move candidates to make compliant with new open data, content, and web API policy.		•		
2.2	Agencies	Make high-value data and content in at least existing two major customer-facing systems available through web APIs, apply metadata tagging and publish a plan to transition additional high-value systems. *[Within 6 months of release of open data policy—see milestone 1.1]*				•
2.3	GSA	Expand Data.gov to include a web API catalog that centrally aggregates web APIs posted on agencies'/developer pages.				•
PART B: Shared Platform						
3. Establish a Digital Services Innovation Center and Advisory Group						
3.1	GSA	Establish a Digital Services Innovation Center to improve the government's delivery of digital services.	•			
3.2	OMB	Convene a Digital Services Advisory Group to prioritize Innovation Center activities and help develop government-wide best practices, guidance, and standards.	•			
3.3	Advisory Group/ Federal CIO Council	Release government-wide bring-your-own-device (BYOD) guidance based on lessons learned from successful pilots at federal agencies.		•		
3.4	Innovation Center	Identify shared and open content management system solutions.			•	
3.5	Innovation Center	Provide support to help agencies develop web APIs.			•	
3.6	Innovation Center/ Federal CIO Council	Launch a shared mobile app development program.				•

#	Owner(s)	Milestone Actions	Timeframe (months)			
			1	3	6	12
Part B: Shared Platform (cont.)						
4. Establish Intra-Agency Governance to Improve Delivery of Digital Services						
4.1	Advisory Group	Recommend guidelines on agency-wide governance structure for developing and delivering digital services.		•		
4.2	Agencies	Establish an agency-wide governance structure for developing and delivering digital services. [*Within 3 months of release of governance guidance—see milestone 4.1*]			•	
5. Shift to an Enterprise-Wide Asset Management and Procurement Model						
5.1	GSA	Establish government-wide contract vehicle for mobile devices and wireless service.			•	
5.2	Agencies	Develop an enterprise-wide inventory of mobile devices and wireless service contracts.			•	
5.3	Agencies	Evaluate the government-wide contract vehicles in the alternatives analysis for all new mobile-related procurements.				•
5.4	Advisory Group/ Federal CIO Council	Develop models for the delivery of commercial mobile applications into the federal environment.				•
5.5	GSA	Set up a government-wide mobile device management platform.				•
Part C: Customer-Centric						
6. Deliver Better Digital Services Using Modern Tools and Technologies						
6.1	Advisory Group/ Federal Web Managers Council	Recommend guidelines for improving digital services and customer experience.			•	
6.2	GSA	Update the dot gov domain guidance and procedures to help ensure all new digital services meet improvement guidelines and provide support to agencies.			•	
6.3	Agencies	Ensure all new digital services follow digital services and customer experience improvement guidelines. [*Within 6 months of release of improvement guidance—see milestone 6.2*]				•
7. Improve Priority Customer Facing Services for Mobile Use						
7.1	Agencies	Engage with customers to identify at least two existing priority customer-facing services to optimize for mobile use.		•		
7.2	Agencies	Optimize at least two existing priority customer-facing services for mobile use and publish a plan for improving additional existing services. [*Within 6 months of release of digital services improvement guidance—see milestone 6.2*]				•

#	Owner(s)	Milestone Actions	Timeframe (months)			
			1	3	6	12
Part C: Customer-Centric (cont.)						
8. Measure Performance and Customer Satisfaction to Improve Service Delivery						
8.1	Innovation Center	Provide tools and guidance for measuring performance and customer satisfaction on digital services.		•		
8.2	Agencies	Implement performance and customer satisfaction measuring tools on all .gov websites. *[Within 3 months of release of tools and guidance—see milestone 8.1]*			•	
Part D: Security and Privacy						
9. Promote the Safe and Secure Adoption of New Technologies						
9.1	DHS/DOD/ NIST	Develop government-wide mobile and wireless security base-line (includes security reference architectures.)	'			•
10. Evaluate and Streamline Security and Privacy Processes						
10.1	NIST	Report on NIST's ongoing work in mobile technology, including the applicability of NIST's standards and guidelines to mobile devices and platforms.		•		
10.2	Advisory Group/ Federal CIO Council	Evaluate opportunities to accelerate the secure adoption of mobile technologies into the federal environment at reduced cost.			•	
10.3	Federal CIO Council/NIST/ NARA	Develop guidelines for standardized implementation of digital privacy controls and educate agency privacy and legal officials on options for addressing digital privacy, records retention, and security issues.			•